The GORSKI–CENAPS® MODEL for Recovery and Relapse Prevention

The GORSKI–CENAPS® MODEL for Recovery and Relapse Prevention

Developed by
Terence T. Gorski, President
The CENAPS® Corporation

A Comprehensive Overview of a Research-Based System That Works

This booklet describes The GORSKI-CENAPS® Model for Recovery and Relapse Prevention and the research on which it was based. An initial paper titled "The CENAPS® Model Relapse Prevention Therapy (RPT): A Description of Counseling Approaches" was developed for the National Institute on Drug Abuse (NIDA) Study to Identify and Describe Drug Abuse Counseling Approaches. Terence T. Gorski, president of The CENAPS® Corporation, developed this paper. The original paper was submitted to Kathleen M. Carroll, Ph.D., assistant professor of psychiatry, director of psychotherapy research, Division of Substance Abuse, Department of Psychiatry School of Medicine. In 1993 Terence T. Gorski copyrighted the original paper before it was submitted to the NIDA. Full permission was granted by the copyright holder for the NIDA to reproduce and distribute that paper.

The original paper was also submitted on April 30, 1993, to Diane Clark of the Infinity Conference Group Incorporated: 11781 Lee Jackson Highway, Suite 185, Fairfax, VA 22033.

Additional copies are available from the publisher:
Herald House/Independence Press
1001 West Walnut
P.O. Box 390
Independence, MO 64051-0390
Phone: 1-800-767-8181 or (816) 521-3015
Fax: (816) 521-3066
Web site: *www.relapse.org*

Notice of Proprietary Information: This booklet contains copyrighted and proprietary information of Terence T. Gorski and The CENAPS® Corporation. Its receipt or possession does not convey any right to reproduce it; to disclose its contents; or to manufacture, use, or sell anything it may describe. Reproduction, disclosure, and use without the specific written authorization of The CENAPS® Corporation are strictly forbidden. If you would like the rights to use any part of this material, please contact The CENAPS® Corporation, 6147 Deltona Blvd., Spring Hill, FL 34606, to discuss the arrangements necessary to make that possible. Phone: (352) 596-8000, fax: (352) 596-8002, Web site: *www.cenaps.com,* or e-mail: *info@cenaps.com.*

© 2007 Terence T. Gorski
ISBN: 978-0-8309-1326-8

Printed in the United States of America

Contents

Foreword 6
Overview of the GORSKI-CENAPS® Model
Part 1
   1.1   General Description 10
   1.2   Research Basis 10
   1.3   Target Population 17
   1.4   Adaptation to Special Populations 18
   1.5   Levels of Clinical Application 19
   1.6   Counselor Characteristics 21
   1.7   Compatibility with Other Models and Standards .. 26
   1.8   Compatibility with Standards 30
   1.9   Setting of Treatment 30
   1.10 Duration of Treatment 31

Part 2
   2.1   Conceptual Models of the GORSKI-CENAPS® System 35
   2.2   Biopsychosocial Model of Addiction 35
   2.3   Developmental Model of Recovery 37
   2.4   Relapse Prevention Model 39
   2.5   Cognitive, Affective, Behavorial, Social (CABS) Therapy 39
   2.6   Treatment-Planning Components 41
   2.7   Helping Characteristics 43
   2.8   Interviewing Skills 45
   2.9   Treatment Delivery Systems 46
   2.10 Strategies for Dealing with Common Clinical Problems 54

The GORSKI-CENAPS® Corporation 58
References 59
Bibliography 64

Foreword
By Terence T. Gorski

It was a cold Friday night on the near north side of Chicago. It was late September in 1970. I remember that night clearly. I was huddled down over a cup of coffee in a greasy-spoon restaurant on the corner of Clark Street and Webster Avenue. I was twenty years old and talking with my best friend, Joe Troiani.

We were both working as psychiatric assistants at Grant Hospital of Chicago and taking intensive training in addiction psychotherapy from Richard Weedman, the director of the hospital's addiction program. The training was working. My emotions were stirred up. My motivation was high. My mind was working in a state of creative overdrive.

As I sat there, I realized that the past year of clinical training and practical experiences had brought me into a new world. I was just beginning to explore that world and learn how to talk about it with trusted friends. Pieces of new knowledge and systems for personal growth were clashing in my mind. I was struggling to organize what I was learning.

Three different bodies of knowledge were in competition: my college psychology courses taught by Dr. Stan Martindale, a former student of Carl Rogers; my intensive training in addiction psychotherapy with Richard Weedman, who would later draft the first standards for addiction treatment for the Joint Commission for the Accreditation of Hospitals; and the practical applied therapies and Twelve-Step recovery methods I was using with clients in the combined addiction and psychiatric unit of Grant Hospital.

I could sense the value of all three perspectives, but something was missing. I needed a higher perspective—a bigger frame of reference that could organize this information into a practical system. I knew a lot, but I was struggling to figure out how to apply what I was learning in the real world of treatment and recovery.

On that cold night in September, a vision of how to do this came together in my mind. This was a moment of clarity—a peak experience that Fritz Pearls called "the Aha moment" and many people in Twelve-Step programs call "a blinding flash of the obvious." As I struggled to explain this vision to Joe, I found myself at a loss for words. The vision was general and I lacked the words to explain the sense of knowing that seemed to have reorganized the very circuits of my brain. But the vision was there. From that moment, I didn't have the vision; the vision had me. I didn't know it then, but this vision would shape the rest of my professional career and personal life.

At first the vision was poorly articulated. It was a sense of how to build a containing framework that would allow the information and skills I was learning to come together in a practical and effective way. It was the idea of building *a higher order model of addiction treatment.*

This model, which would slowly evolve into the CENAPS® Model for Recovery and Relapse Prevention, would have to be big enough to include and integrate the major therapeutic approaches to addiction. The vision was to create an effective and easy-to-use system that integrated the physical, psychological, social, and spiritual aspects of recovery. Most importantly, the model needed to be a living, growing, and evolving system capable of integrating new research information as it became available.

To do this, the model needed a simple, no-nonsense language that eliminated psychological jargon, complex research abstractions, and recovery clichés. This no-nonsense language, however, would need to maintain a clear focus on the core issues of how to recover from addiction and avoid relapse. It would need to clearly describe practical methods that could work in the real world.

As a result of this conversation with a trusted friend on that cold night, I developed the conviction that such a system could be developed and taught to both therapists and recovering people. I was convinced that it could include the rich and effective therapeutic systems that had evolved over time, while transcending their limitations. I knew this system could open up a bigger frame of reference that would provide new and more effective approaches to recovery and relapse prevention.

Although the vision was vividly clear in my own mind, describing it and developing the supportive materials became a lifelong work. As I began using these new ideas with clients, the system took on greater clarity. Concrete recovery exercises were developed that evolved into a flexible system of manualized treatment.

The description of this system emerged from the training sessions that I conducted with both recovering people and multidisciplinary treatment professionals. Since the training sessions were skill oriented and experiential, I usually learned as much from the students as they did from me. Each time I did a training workshop, it integrated new research, knowledge, and understandings I had gathered since the last experience. The training was designed to help participants connect their real-lived experiences, both professionally and personally, to the practical methods of recovery and relapse prevention that were part of the CENAPS® Model. The responses were usually positive, and most people attending the advanced skills training sessions started adapting and using various parts of the model in their work with addicts in the real world. They reported that they saw dramatic changes in how their clients responded to treatment and recovery.

As the training handouts grew into training manuals and the manuals grew into books, the model expanded in its scope. Over time the CENAPS® Model focused on the critical path of recovery. It shrugged off a lot of interesting but unnecessary information and recovery tasks that could sidetrack the treatment and recovery process.

Over the years I have published many books and articles describing aspects of the CENAPS® Model. Looking through the CENAPS catalog and our Web site, *www.relapse.org,* you can see the wealth of information that has been made available. However, there has always been one vital publication that has been missing—a concise overview of the entire CENAPS® Model.

I have been working on this description for years, yet I never felt the model was complete. I viewed it as a work in progress, and I still do. So I was reluctant to commit myself to publishing an overall description I knew would grow and change as more research and experience became available. Recently, I was persuaded by my colleagues that a decisive overview of the entire model was necessary. I was convinced that many people were using a small piece of the CENAPS® Model and were not even aware that other components of the model existed.

As a result, I have published this comprehensive overview of the CENAPS® Model. This resource is meant to provide an overview of the entire system and show how the different parts of the system work together. The CENAPS® Model is also being expanded to address related mental health problems including depression, suicide, and antisocial behaviors.

It is exciting for me to look back over the last thirty years and see a vision of a recovery system become a reality that is helping people in the United States, Iceland, England, Denmark, Sweden, Hungary, and many other countries around the world. Today, there are more than 3,000 professionals trained in the GORSKI-CENAPS® Model for Recovery and Relapse Prevention. I will continue devoting my energies to the refinement of the CENAPS® Model and its systematic application to a broad spectrum of behavioral health and societal problems. I hope you will enjoy and benefit from an understanding of the current state of the model and that this understanding will help you use its individual components more effectively.

Overview of the GORSKI-CENAPS® Model Part 1

1.1 General Description

The GORSKI-CENAPS® Model for Recovery and Relapse Prevention is a comprehensive system for diagnosing and treating substance use disorders and coexisting mental disorders, personality disorders, and situational life problems. The model is based on a biopsychosocial model of addiction, a developmental model of recovery, and a relapse prevention model. The model integrates addiction-specific treatment methods with state-of-the-art cognitive, affective, behavioral, and social therapies.

1.2 Research Basis

The GORSKI-CENAPS® Model is a research-based system. It is evolutionary because it includes the strengths of a wide variety of clinical models while transcending their limitations. The GORSKI-CENAPS® Model is dynamic because it is designed to grow by integrating new research findings while adapting to current fiscal constraints. The model is designed to be used in cross-disciplinary environment staffed by multidisciplinary treatment providers. Because the model uses plain, no-nonsense language whenever possible and it seeks to avoid professional jargon, it can be easily adapted to the personal, clinical style of therapists and program managers while meeting the individualized recovery needs of clients. Today there are over 3,000 professionals trained in the GORSKI-CENAPS® Model for Recovery and Relapse Prevention.

The research basis that supports the model comes from a variety of different sources.
- **Clinical Modeling:** The original version of the GORSKI-CENAPS® Model was developed based on direct observations of the phenomena of addiction, recovery, and re-

lapse. Direct clinical experiences with addicted patients at three different centers provided observation of the symptomatology of addiction at various stages of severity, the recovery process over periods of up to two years of outpatient treatment, and the relapse process. These observations were carefully documented and synthesized into a descriptive model.

- **Literature Reviews:** Ongoing literature reviews were conducted starting in 1973, and new research advances were carefully integrated into various components of the model.

- **Single Case Research Studies:** Over one thousand relapse prevention case studies, which demonstrate that over 80 percent of the cases managed to stop an ongoing series of progressive relapse episodes, were conducted in accordance with the National Relapse Prevention Certification School.

- **Outcome Studies:** Several outcome studies were conducted by treatment programs using the GORSKI-CENAPS® Model and compared to the outcomes of other programs. These studies consistently showed that overall abstinence of between 60 and 80 percent were achieved after one year, and relapse-prone clients were able to achieve outcomes as a result of relapse prevention programs that were equal to clients completing treatment for the first time.

- **Controlled Studies:** An NIDA study by Miller[1] on Gorski's relapse warning signs was conducted and showed that these warning signs were highly predictive of relapse.

There are three primary theoretical models on which the GORSKI-CENAPS® Model is constructed. They are the Biopsychosocial Model of Substance Use Disorders, the Development Model of Recovery, and the Relapse Prevention Model. Each of these components is built on a solid foundation of research studies.

Biopsychosocial Model: The Biopsychosocial Model of Addiction is based on an integration of four science-based models of addiction: Neuropsychological Predisposition Model, Neuropsychological Response Model, Social Learning Model, and Cognitive Therapy Model of Substance Abuse. The components of these models have been translated into simple language and carefully integrated for consistency. The basic research-based components of these models will be briefly explained so their application with the GORSKI-CENAPS® Model can be easily recognized.

1. Neuropsychological Predisposition Model:[2] The Neuropsychological Predisposition Model describes *the preexisting brain and central nervous system problems* that increase the risk of becoming addicted. These predisposing neuropsychological risk factors may be related to genetically inherited traits, brain dysfunction caused by improper prenatal care, the effects of prenatal alcohol or drug use, physical neglect (the absence of touching, rocking, and responsive, loving human interaction) or abuse in early infancy, severe psychological trauma experienced at different points in childhood, and adolescent development.

These preexisting neuropsychological problems make people more vulnerable or susceptible to abuse and addiction to alcohol and other drugs and make them susceptible (i.e., less resistant) to the damaging effects of alcohol and drugs to the brain. These preexisting problems are usually exacerbated by alcohol and drug use and interfere with efforts to stop drinking and using drugs.

These predisposing neuropsychological problems are: (1) the tendency to have severe mood swings; (2) difficulty in concentrating; (3) difficulty persisting in tasks through completion; (4) impulse-control problems; (5) the tendency to be hyperactive and irritable; and (6) cognitive impairments that interfere with self-awareness, awareness of the immediate environment, abstract reasoning, problem solving, learning from past experiences, and the logical consequences of current behavior to anticipate and avoid future problems.

The early research basis of this neurobehavioral model was the analysis of 139 supportive scientific studies.[3]

2. Neuropsychological Response Model of Addiction:[4]

The Neuropsychological Response Model describes *the primary reactions of the brain and nervous system to the ingestion of alcohol and drugs* that motivate people to keep using in progressively greater amounts and to have difficulty stopping even after serious problems develop.

People start drinking and using drugs as a result of personal curiosity, being motivated by social pressure to use alcohol or drugs, and the availability of these substances.

- **Neurobiological Reinforcement:** People at high risk of addiction experience neurobiological reinforcement when they use alcohol or other drugs because the substances activate brain chemistry responses that cause a state of euphoria that is experienced as a unique sense of pleasure and well being. This feeling of euphoria acts as a positive reinforcement that motivates people to keep using alcohol or other drugs.

- **Tolerance:** People at high risk of addiction develop tolerance when they start using alcohol and other drugs regularly and heavily. Tolerance occurs as neurochemical processes in the brain adapt to the presence of alcohol and drugs in a way that allows people to feel and function normally when using. This means they need to use progressively larger amounts of alcohol and drugs in order to experience the desired euphoric response. The combination of neurobiological reinforcement and tolerance motivates people to use progressively larger amounts of alcohol and drugs more and more frequently.

- **Physical Dependence:** When people at high risk of addiction use alcohol and drugs frequently and heavily, they develop a physical dependence. This is because their brain requires certain amounts of alcohol or drugs to function normally. If the amount of alcohol and drugs needed for normal functioning is not provided, they experience withdrawal symptoms caused by brain chemistry imbalances. This creates a state of emotional distress that makes it difficult to function normally. There are two distinct withdrawal syndromes: *acute withdrawal,* which occurs immediately after the cessation of alcohol and drug use; and *post acute withdrawal,* which persists for a prolonged period of time after the cessation of alcohol and drug use. Alcohol and drug withdrawal motivates people to start using alcohol and drugs when they try to stop. Acute withdrawal produces immediate and severe symptoms prompting a return to substance use within hours or days of attempting to stop. Post acute withdrawal produces a chronic state of low grade agitated depression accompanied by difficulty in thinking clearly, a tendency to swing between episodes of emotional overreaction and emotional numbness, difficulties with impulse control, and problems with self-motivation. These symptoms become more severe during periods of high stress. Post acute withdrawal motivates people to start using alcohol and drugs during periods of high stress after the acute withdrawal has subsided.

- **Progressive Brain Dysfunction:** People who become addicted develop progressive brain dysfunction that can become so severe it meets the criteria of a *substance-induced organic mental disorder.* This severe brain dysfunction creates an inability to meet major life responsibilities, and, in its severe form, disrupts the ability to perform normal acts of daily living.

The early research basis of this neurobiological model was the analysis of 160 supportive scientific studies.[5]

3. **Social Learning Model:** This learning model is based on extensive evidence that the development of addiction to alcohol and other drugs is related to *a complex interaction among a variety of personal, interpersonal, and environmental factors* that motivate people to use alcohol and drugs to cope with a wide variety of experiences. These factors and their relationship can be summarized as follows:

Vicarious Learning: People learn a set of self-regulatory responses to alcohol and drugs by observing other people and events around them. These self-regulatory responses are initially learned in childhood and are either reinforced or challenged as a result of critical developmental and other life experiences. These self-regulatory responses include

- *beliefs* about alcohol and drug use;
- *behavioral skills* for acquiring and using alcohol and drugs;
- *self-monitoring skills* for observing drinking and drugging behavior;
- *judgmental skills* for evaluating the benefits and disadvantages associated with alcohol and drug use;
- *self-rewarding behaviors* used when alcohol and drug use conforms with a person's beliefs and values; and
- *self-punishing behaviors* used when a person's alcohol and drug use does not conform to their beliefs and coping skills for dealing with the consequences of their alcohol and drug use.

Personal Experience with Alcohol and Drug Use: People have initial experiences with alcohol and drugs, use the learned self-regulatory responses, and develop a set of positive memories associated with alcohol and drug use.

Positive Expectancy: People may develop the belief that the use of alcohol and drugs will produce positive or reinforcing outcomes and come to anticipate and expect these outcomes.

Conditioned Craving: Specific experiences or sensory triggers become associated with the reinforcing effects of alcohol and drugs and when experienced they activate a craving or urge to use alcohol and drugs.

Adaptation of Self-Regulatory Processes: People may slowly adapt their self-regulatory responses in order to maximize positive reinforcement and minimize negative reinforcement. This involves the development of distorted perceptions and irrational ways of thinking that support a positive belief about alcohol and drug use despite the presence of progressive, more severe adverse consequences.

Self-Reinforcing Addiction Cycle: A self-reinforcing addiction cycle may develop that locks a person into a pattern of progressively more dysfunctional cognitions and behaviors.

> *The early research basis of this social learning model was the analysis of 111 supportive scientific studies.*[6]

4. Cognitive Therapy of Substance Abuse: The GORSKI-CENAPS® Model is fully consistent with cognitive therapy principles for substance abuse treatment.[7,8] The Cognitive Model of Substance Abuse is based on the observation that substance abusers develop a set of irrational beliefs that support their ongoing use of alcohol and drugs while blocking out or minimizing the importance of problems caused by their use. Treatment is based on establishing a collaborative relationship with the client and helping them to identify and challenge these basic addictive beliefs.

> *Aaron Beck provides 239 scientific references that support the Cognitive Therapy Model of Substance Abuse Treatment. Albert Ellis provides 139 scientific references that support the application of Rational Emotive Therapy (RET) to the treatment of substance abusers.*

The features of these four models were translated into common language and integrated into a general framework of the earlier phenomenologically developed model to provide the basic form and structure of the current GORSKI-CENAPS® Model. The model was later updated to assure its consistency with a more recent biopsychosocial analysis of addiction.

> *This early research was based on the analysis of 49 supportive scientific studies.*[9]

5. Developmental Model of Recovery (DMR)

The Developmental Model of Recovery was initially developed from the observations of clients' recoveries over the course of two years of outpatient substance abuse treatment. This model was first published as a chapter in a recovery education book in 1982,[10] as a training manual in 1985,[11] and by Hazelden in 1989.[12]

The Developmental Model of Recovery used in the GORSKI-CENAPS® Model is consistent with the Stages of Change Model developed by Prochaska and Diclemente[13] and the Developmental Model of Recovery developed by Stephanie Brown.[14]

6. Relapse Prevention Model

The Relapse Prevention Model is consistent with the original cognitive model of relapse prevention[15] and state-of-the-art relapse prevention methods described in *Substance Abuse: A Comprehensive Textbook*.[16] Relapse prevention has been demonstrated to be effective by a number of research studies. A meta-analysis (Bowers et al., 1999) was performed to evaluate the overall effectiveness of relapse prevention and the extent to which certain variables may relate to treatment outcome. Twenty-six published and unpublished studies with seventy hypothesis tests representing a sample of 9,504 participants were included in the analysis. Results indicated that relapse prevention was generally effective, especially for clients with alcohol and drug problems.[17]

1.3 Target Population

The patients who do well with the GORSKI-CENAPS® Model are the same types of patients who do well with other cognitive-behavioral addiction treatment approaches. The model also does extremely well with clients who have been previously treated with other addiction treatment models and

have relapsed. The general characteristics of patients who do well are those who
- have average or above average conceptual skills;
- have sixth grade or above reading and writing skills;
- are currently abstinent from alcohol and other drugs and free of the symptoms of acute alcohol and drug withdrawal; and
- do not have severe learning disabilities, cognitive impairments, or other active psychiatric symptoms that interfere with the ability to participate in a structured cognitive-behavioral therapy program.

Patients who do not do well with the GORSKI-CENAPS® Model are those with severely impaired conceptual abilities, significant literacy problems, serious organic impairments that interfere with the ability to learn and process information, learning disabilities, or other mental disorders that interfere with their ability to respond to cognitive behavioral therapy interventions.

1.4 Adaptation to Special Populations

The GORSKI-CENAPS® Model has been adapted to meet the needs of a variety of patient populations including the following:
- Patients addicted to a variety of mind-altering substances including alcohol, sedatives, sleeping pills, stimulants (such as cocaine, methamphetamine, and amphetamine), narcotics (such as heroine, Demerol, and codeine), psychedelic drugs (such as LSD), and club drugs
- Adults
- Adolescents
- Families
- Addicted patients with pain disorders
- Relapse-prone African Americans
- Relapse-prone Native Americans

- Addicted patients with coexisting eating disorders
- Revolving door, indigent detox patients
- Physically and sexually abused men and women
- Addicted offenders in the criminal justice system both behind bars and under community supervision
- Addicted patients with a wide variety of coexisting Axis I Psychiatric Disorders (after debilitating initial symptoms have been stabilized with medication)
- Addicted patients with a wide variety of coexisting Axis II Personality Disorders

1.5 Levels of Clinical Application

The GORSKI-CENAPS® Model is designed to be used on one of two levels:

Level 1—The Counseling Level: Patients need to learn new ways of thinking and acting that will allow them to manage high-risk situations and other problems that occur in their lives without using alcohol or drugs. The primary focus is to teach the client how to do something different when they encounter these situations. Patients are taught to identify and more effectively manage the thoughts and feelings that get in the way of learning new and more effective ways of dealing with problem situations.

Level 2—The Psychotherapy Level: These situations are created by repetitive self-defeating behaviors that are motivated by core personality and lifestyle problems. These basic mistaken beliefs about self, others, and the world motivate clients to become involved in and mismanage high-risk situations despite their conscious intent not to.

- *Core personality problems* are self-defeating habits of thinking, feeling, acting, and relating to others.
- *Core lifestyle problems* are the habitual ways of living and the agreements and relationships we establish with other people at work, in the community, and

with friends, family, and lovers. These core lifestyle problems are a social structure that both supports and justifies the personality problems.

There are two different types of treatment designed to address these two different levels of client problems.

Counseling: Counseling is the process of teaching clients how to identify and manage high-risk situations and to identify and change the patterns of thinking, feeling, and acting that prevent them from effectively managing the situation. This is called *Relapse Prevention Counseling*.

Psychotherapy: Psychotherapy is the process of teaching clients how to identify and manage the core personality and lifestyle problems that cause them to keep putting themselves in high-risk situations. It then teaches them how to identify and change the core belief systems and unconscious life rules that create and maintain their personality and lifestyle. This is called *Relapse Prevention Therapy*.

The GORSKI-CENAPS® Model has components that can address both levels of problems, but it is recommended that clinicians working at the psychotherapy level have a background in both addiction counseling and advanced clinical training in psychotherapy.

The following general decision rules are applied for determining when to work at the counseling or psychotherapy level:

- Clients must be able to stay abstinent from alcohol and drugs before they can successfully work on psychotherapy issues.

- Clients should be able to identify and manage high-risk situations at a counseling level without using alcohol or drugs before moving into psychotherapy.

- Focusing treatment on core personality and lifestyle issues can defocus clients from identifying and managing high-risk situations that can cause alcohol and drug use.

As a result, a premature focus upon psychotherapy can increase the risk of relapse.

- Working on the psychotherapy issues can also increase pain and stress. This makes it even more difficult for the client to manage the high-risk situation.

- Every high-risk situation is like the tip of an iceberg. It sits on top of a cluster of underlying personality and lifestyle problems. These underlying problems often surface when the client starts learning how to identify and manage the high-risk situation.

- It is often difficult to keep the client focused on learning how to manage the high-risk situation when these deeper issues get activated. The client wants to focus on the deeper issue because it is easier to look at psychotherapy issues than to focus on learning basic abstinence skills. Since these issues are real and cause the client pain and discomfort, the counselor often feels obligated to work on these issues.

- It is inappropriate to ignore core personality and lifestyle issues or communicate to the client that these issues are not important. The client will have to resolve these issues if they are to learn how to maintain long-term abstinence. The issue is that there are other immediate situations that represent an immediate risk to abstinence. These issues must be dealt with first. Later we will review a technique called *bookmarking* that will allow us to honor core personality and lifestyle issues as they come while keeping the primary focus on identifying and managing the high-risk situations that can cause alcohol and drug use.

1.6 Counselor Characteristics

Educational Requirements: Professionals with a variety of degree credentials, ranging from nondegreed certified addiction counselors to doctoral level clinical psychologists, have been trained and successfully practice the GORSKI-

CENAPS® Model for Relapse Prevention Therapy. The more training in chemical dependency treatment and cognitive behavioral therapy, the more effective the clinician is in utilizing the GORSKI-CENAPS® Model.

As a general rule, certified addiction counselors, without baccalaureate-level degrees, utilize the model at the counseling level under the supervision of a certified addiction counselor with a master's or doctoral degree. The advanced psychotherapy approaches are often restricted to certified addiction counselors with a master's degree or equivalent experience.

Training, Credentials, and Experience: Many counselors and therapists are able to use GORSKI-CENAPS® Model techniques effectively after reading published literature on the model. Many programs, for example, have installed relapse prevention programs based on *Staying Sober: A Guide for Relapse Prevention, The Staying Sober Workbook,* and the *Staying Sober Recovery Education Modules.* Newer publications have updated and expanded the GORSKI-CENAPS® Model into a wider range of application. The *Denial Management Counseling (DMC) Workbook* and the *Denial Management Counseling (DMC) Professional Guide* have focused the model on the needs of clients with strong denial and treatment resistance. The *Relapse Prevention Counseling (RPC) Workbook* has expanded the model into specific applications of managing high-risk situations. The *Relapse Prevention Therapy (RPT) Workbook* focuses on the identification and management of core personality and lifestyle problems that lead to relapse later in recovery after initial stabilization has been achieved. The *Addiction-Free Pain Management Workbook* and its related *Addiction-Free Pain Management Professional Guide* apply the model to special needs of recovering people with chronic pain disorders and people who have become addicted to prescription pain medication. These and other materials clearly outline the basic theories and clinical procedures and provide patient materials for implementation. Clinical skill-training programs and an optional competency certification procedure are available for most components.

Counselor Recovery Status: Whether a counselor is in recovery from addiction or not is irrelevant to the delivery of the GORSKI-CENAPS® Model for Relapse Prevention Therapy. It is important that the therapist believe in abstinence-based treatment, avoid the use of harsh psychonoxious confrontation, have good communication skills, have well-developed helping characteristics, and be able to role model a functional and sober lifestyle. The capacity for empathy with the relapse-prone patient is essential.

Ideal Personal Characteristics of the Counselor: Ideally, therapists using the GORSKI-CENAPS® Model would be recovering chemically dependent people who recovered using GORSKI-CENAPS® therapy methods, who currently have over five years of uninterrupted sobriety, and have earned a master's degree or above with advanced training in cognitive, affective, and behavioral therapy techniques.

Therapist Behaviors: The GORSKI-CENAPS® Model trains therapists to enter into a collaborative relationship with their patients and use supportive and directive approaches which avoid harsh confrontation. Therapists need to have the ability to clearly set and firmly enforce limits while avoiding the extremes. One extreme to be avoided is becoming overly controlling and punitive. Another extreme to be avoided is becoming overly compliant with the client's demands and using enabling behaviors. A foundation of good basic counseling and therapy skills are required.

Role of the Counselor/Therapist: The counselor or therapist plays the role of educator, collaborator, and therapist. The counselor has a prescribed series of recovery and relapse prevention exercises that guide a patient through the context of group and individual therapy sessions and structured psychoeducation programs. The goal is to explain each procedure or exercise, assign appropriate homework preparation, and process the results of the exercise in group and individual therapy. The goal is to help patients recognize and manage relapse warning signs by facilitating insight, catharsis, and behavior change.

Role of the Patient/Client: The patient is expected to play an active role in the relapse prevention therapy process. The patient is given a series of assignments and is expected to actively process those assignments in group and individual therapy sessions. Many of the assignments involve peer support and sharing of information and experiences.

Typical Sessions: The GORSKI-CENAPS® Model uses structured problem-solving group therapy, individual therapy, and psychoeducational session formats. Patients are asked to make a commitment to a structured recovery program including self-help groups and holistic health programs that include proper diet, exercise, and social and spiritual activities.

Topics or Themes: Therapy is primarily directed toward the identification and management of relapse warning signs. This model consists of structured exercises that have been developed with over twenty years of clinical experience. These are presented in detail in *The Staying Sober Workbook*, *Relapse Prevention Therapy Workbook*, and *Counseling for Relapse Prevention*.

Manualized Treatment (Patient Workbooks): The most effective treatment programs utilize a manualized clinical system that includes reading assignments, journal assignments, self-assessment questionnaires, and preparation assignments for group and individual therapy sessions. Effective manualized treatment needs to match the content of treatment manuals and the modalities in which the content is processed with the problems of the client.

The primary focus of all sessions is to guide the patient in the completion of structured exercises contained in a patient workbook. The following workbooks are available: *Denial Management Counseling Workbook*, *Relapse Prevention Counseling: Practical Exercises for Managing High-Risk Situations*, *Relapse Prevention Therapy Workbook: Managing Core Personality and Lifestyle Issues*, *Addiction-Free Pain Management*, *Food Addiction: Recovery and Relapse Prevention Workbook*, and others. A process has been developed for custom designing treatment manuals (i.e., client workbooks) that address specific recurrent issues within treatment programs.

All applications of the GORSKI-CENAPS® Model rely on the use of core clinical skills directed at teaching clients specific recovery skills. The basic recovery skills that are adapted to each level of a patient's recovery follow:

Introspection Skills: The ability to identify self-talk, feelings and emotions, and urges to act

Social Awareness Skills: The ability to observe and accurately assess the behavior of others

Cognitive Skills: The ability to identify and challenge addictive and irrational forms of thinking

Affective Skills: The ability to recognize feelings and emotions, accurately describe them in words, and communicate them to others when appropriate

Behavioral Skills: Two core behavioral skills are impulse control and self-motivation. Impulse control is the ability to recognize cravings and self-destructive urges and stop acting out on those cravings or urges. Self-motivation is the ability to force oneself to engage in healthy and productive behavior even when you don't want to.

Social Skills: A relationship building model based on levels of relationship is used to guide clients in slowly rebuilding their social network. The core social skills involved in the social rebuilding process are the ability to engage in productive communication using an active listening model, set and enforce appropriate boundaries and limits in social situations, stop using controlling and manipulative behaviors, and engage in negotiation and conflict resolution.

Problem and Warning Sign identification Skills: Identification skills include the ability to identify and develop a personalized list of the unique personal problems that lead the client back to alcohol and drug use (called relapse warning signs) and problem or warning-sign management strategies that consist of concrete situational and behavioral coping strategies for managing the warning signs without returning to chemical use.

Recovery Program Development Skills: Patients are taught how to develop a structured recovery program that provides a regular daily structure for maintaining a healthy and sober lifestyle. Breaks in the recovery program are viewed as critical relapse warning signs, and immediate intervention is initiated when they become apparent.

Amount of Structure: The program is highly structured, and compliance with the basic therapeutic structures is strongly emphasized as a prerequisite for involvement.

1.7 Compatibility with Other Models and Standards

The GORSKI-CENAPS® Model for Treatment of Substance Use Disorders and related personality, mental, and lifestyle problems has been under development since the early 1970s.[18] It integrates the fundamental principles of Alcoholics Anonymous (AA) with the most recent advances in biological, cognitive, affective, behavioral, and social therapies to meet the needs of relapse-prone patients.

The GORSKI-CENAPS® Model can be described as the third wave of chemical dependency treatment. The first wave was the introduction of the Twelve Steps of Alcoholics Anonymous. The second wave was the integration of AA with professional treatment into a model known as the Minnesota Model.

The GORSKI-CENAPS® Model is the third wave in chemical dependency treatment, because it integrates knowledge of chemical dependency into a biopsychosocial model that is compatible with Twelve-Step principles and biological, cognitive, affective, behavioral, and social therapy principles to produce a model for assessment and treatment planning for use during all stages of the recovery process.

The GORSKI-CENAPS® Model is a comprehensive system for diagnosing and treating substance use disorders and related mental disorders, personality disorders, and lifestyle problems. The model has been used successfully since the early 1970s in addiction, mental health, and behavioral health treatment programs.

The GORSKI-CENAPS® Model has been successfully adapted for use in all levels of care with a wide variety of clients including women, adolescents, homosexuals, African Americans, Native Americans, Hispanic Americans, clients with chronic pain, and clients with other coexisting disorders being treated in community mental health centers.

The GORSKI-CENAPS® Model has been translated into a number of languages including Spanish, Polish, Danish, Swedish, Hungarian, Japanese, Korean, Bangla, Russian, Arabic, and Slovenian.

The GORSKI-CENAPS® Model has been used effectively under a wide variety of health-care financing plans, including private insurance, federal funding, state funding, managed care plans, health maintenance organizations, and self-pay private practices.

The reason the GORSKI-CENAPS® Model has survived and thrived under such a variety of financing schemes is because it is based on rock-solid clinical principles that are flexible enough to adapt to changing conditions in the health-care field.

Approaches Most Similar: The GORSKI-CENAPS® Model for Relapse Prevention Therapy is an applied and expanded cognitive-behavioral therapy program that incorporates biological and social treatment. Its cognitive components are similar to Albert Ellis's Rational Emotive Therapy (RET) and Aaron Beck's Cognitive Therapy Model. Its affective components are similar to Affective and Experiential Therapies, and its social interventions are built on family systems therapy and the public health model. The primary difference between the GORSKI-CENAPS® Model and the other forms of therapy is that the GORSKI-CENAPS® Model applies cognitive-behavioral therapy principles directly to the problem of treating substance-use disorders and teaching chemically dependent patients and their families how to maintain abstinence from alcohol and drugs.

The GORSKI-CENAPS® Model for Relapse Prevention Therapy heavily emphasizes affective therapy principles by focusing on the identification, appropriate labeling, and communication and resolution of feelings and emotions. The GORSKI-CENAPS® Model integrates a cognitive and affective therapy model for understanding emotions by teaching patients that emotions are generated by irrational thinking (cognitive theory) and are traumatically stored or repressed (affective theory). Emotional integration work involves both cognitive labeling and expression of feelings, and imagery-oriented therapies designed to surface repressed memories. The model relies heavily on guided imagery, spontaneous imagery, sentence completion, and sentence-repetition work designed to create corrective emotional experiences.

This model is similar to and has been heavily influenced by the Cognitive-Behavioral Relapse Prevention Model developed by Marlatt and Gordon.[19, 20] The major difference is that The GORSKI-CENAPS® Model integrates abstinence-based treatment and has greater compatibility with Twelve-Step programs than the Marlatt and Gordon Model.

The GORSKI-CENAPS® Model integrates well with a variety of cognitive, affective, behavioral, and social therapies. Its primary strength is that this model allows clinicians from varying clinical backgrounds to apply their skills directly to relapse prevention. As a result, it is ideal for use by a multidisciplinary treatment team.

Approaches Most Different: The GORSKI-CENAPS® Model for Relapse Prevention Therapy is most dissimilar to the following types of therapy: (1) those that view chemical dependency as a symptom of an underlying mental or psychological problem; (2) controlled drinking or self-control training that promotes controlled or responsible use for chemically dependent patients who have exhibited physical and psychological dependence on alcohol and other drugs; (3) nondirective or client-centered approaches; (4) and any form of therapy that isolates or exclusively focuses on any single domain of physical, psychological, or social functioning to the exclusion of the other domains of functioning.

The GORSKI-CENAPS® Model is very different from rigid cognitive therapy models that believe the challenging of irrational thoughts will bring automatic emotional integration, or rigid affective therapy models that believe emotional catharsis will automatically cause spontaneous cognitive and behavioral changes.

Compatibility with Other Treatments: The GORSKI-CENAPS® Model is compatible with a variety of other treatments including Twelve-Step programs, family therapy, and a variety of cognitive, affective, and behavioral therapy models.

The GORSKI-CENAPS® Model also works well with court drug-diversion programs and employee assistance programs.

A special Occupation Relapse Prevention Protocol has been developed for use in conjunction with EAP program referrals that focus on the identification of on-the-job relapse warning signs and teach EAP counselors and supervisors how to intervene upon those warning signs as part of the supervision and corrective discipline process.

A special protocol for working with chemically dependent criminal offenders has also been developed that integrates the treatment of criminal thinking and antisocial personality disorders with chemical dependency recovery and relapse prevention methods.

Specialty application of the GORSKI-CENAPS® Model for Relapse Prevention Therapy has also been developed for patients with Post Traumatic Stress Disorder (PTSD) resulting from childhood physical and sexual abuse.[21]

Since the protocol identifies and develops management strategies for a variety of problems that cause relapse, co-existing mental disorders and lifestyle problems are often identified and treated in conjunction with relapse prevention therapy.

A special protocol for family therapy was developed to facilitate family involvement in warning sign identification and management. Johnson-style family intervention methods were adapted for use in a family-oriented Relapse Early Intervention Plan.

1.8 Compatibility with Standards

The GORSKI-CENAPS® Model is fully compatible with DSM IV, ASAM Patient Placement Criteria, the standards of the Joint Commission for the Accreditation of Healthcare Organizations (JCAHO), the standards of CARF, and the Core Counselor Competencies as published by the Center for Substance Abuse Treatment (CSAT), the International Certification and Reciprocity Consortium (IC&RC), and the National Association of Alcohol and Drug Abuse Counselors (NAADAC).

1.9 Setting of Treatment

The GORSKI-CENAPS® Model is designed for implementation across all levels of care. Since it is based on a developmental model of recovery that recognizes the possibility of regression, decomposition, and relapse at any stage of the recovery process, the ability to step up or step down the level of care based on a client's current level of stability is built into the system.

Typically patients are detoxified in a variable length of stay in inpatient or residential programs or highly structured outpatient detoxification programs. During detoxification, the patient is stabilized, assessed, and motivated to continue with the GORSKI-CENAPS® Model for Relapse Prevention Therapy in a primary outpatient program. Severely impaired patients are motivated for transfer to a residential rehabilitation program, therapeutic community program, or halfway-house program dependent on their needs.

Patients who have completed detoxification and are less severely impaired and patients who have successfully completed residential treatment, halfway house, and therapeutic communities are transferred into a primary outpatient program consisting of a minimum of twelve group sessions, ten individual therapy sessions, and six psychoeducational sessions administered over a period of six weeks. Patients with literacy problems, cognitive impairments, or mental and personality disorders usually require longer lengths of stay to complete the therapeutic objectives.

On completion of the primary outpatient program, the patient is transferred into an ongoing group and individual therapy program (four group sessions and two individual sessions per month) to implement the warning sign identification and management procedures and update the relapse prevention plan based on experiences in recovery.

Brief readmission (three to ten days) for residential stabilization may be required should patients return to chemical use or develop severe warning signs that render them out of control and at high risk of returning to chemical use.

The model is well adapted for use in the criminal justice system with chemically dependent criminal offenders who have antisocial personality disorders. In the criminal justice system, the GORSKI-CENAPS® Model for Relapse Prevention Therapy is most effective when integrated with the cognitive-behavioral method for identifying and managing criminal thinking. In such programs, the model needs to be initiated in residential treatment during the last twelve weeks of incarceration, needs to be continued in a halfway setting for a period of three to six months, and must be continued in a primary outpatient program for a minimal period of two years.

1.10 Duration of Treatment

The GORSKI-CENAPS® Model for Relapse Prevention Therapy can be administered in a variety of settings over a variable number of sessions.

Residential Rehabilitation Model: The GORSKI-CENAPS® Model was originally utilized in 28-day residential programs and was administered over a course of twenty 90-minute group therapy sessions, twelve individual therapy sessions, and twenty 90-minute psychoeducational sessions. The protocol was supplemented by involvement in self-help groups. Patients were then transferred into a 90-day outpatient program consisting of twelve 90-minute group therapy sessions (once per week) and six 60-minute individual therapy sessions (twice per month). This was supplemented by attendance at twenty-four Twelve-Step meetings and six Relapse Prevention support groups.

Intensive Outpatient Program: The GORSKI-CENAPS® Model for Relapse Prevention Therapy was later utilized in an intensive outpatient program consisting of ten individual therapy sessions, twelve group therapy sessions, six psychoeducational groups, and attendance at six Twelve-Step meetings and six Relapse Prevention support groups. Patients are then transferred into a 90-day warning-sign-identification-management group consisting of twelve group therapy sessions and six individual therapy sessions and continued involvement in Twelve-Step meetings and Relapse Prevention support groups.

Psychoeducational Programs: The GORSKI-CENAPS® Model has been delivered as a psychoeducational program consisting of between eight and twenty-four education sessions ranging from one and a half to three hours per session. Motivated patients with adequate reading and writing skills have been able to benefit from involvement in these programs. These psychoeducational programs are usually integrated with the residential or primary outpatient programs.

Notes

1. W. R. Miller and R. J. Harris, "Simple Scale of Gorski's Warning Signs for Relapse," *Journal of Studies on Alcohol*, 61(5) (September 2000): 759–765.

2. In the literature this model and its related theories are often called the "neurobehavioral model." Since the model involves the neuropsychological responses that predispose people to rapidly develop serious problems related to alcohol and drug use, I will use the term "neuropsychological predisposition model," because it is more descriptive and helps to distinguish this model from the other models that were integrated into the biopsychosocial model.

3. Ralph E. Tarter, Arthur I. Alterman, and Kathleen L. Edwards, "Neurobehavioral Theory of Alcoholism Etiology," IN: EDS: C.D. Chaudron and D.A. Wilkinson, *Theories on Alcoholism* (Toronto, Canada: Addiction Research Foundation, 1988).

4. In the literature, this model and its related theories are often called the "neurobiological model." Since the model involves the direct neuropsychological responses to alcohol and drug use, I will use the term

"neuropsychological response model," because it is more descriptive and helps distinguish this model from the other models that were integrated into the biopsychosocial model.

5. Boris Tabakoff and Paula L. Hoffman, "A Neurobiological Theory of Alcoholism," IN: EDS: C.D. Chaudron and D.A. Wilkinson, *Theories on Alcoholism* (Toronto, Canada: Addiction Research Foundation, 1988).

6. G. Terence Wilson, "Alcohol Use and Abuse: Social Learning Analysis," IN: IN: EDS: C.D. Chaudron and D.A. Wilkinson, *Theories on Alcoholism* (Toronto, Canada: Addiction Research Foundation, 1988).

7. Aaron T. Beck, Fred D. Wright, Cory F. Newman, and Bruce S. Liese, *Cognitive Therapy of Substance Abuse* (New York: Guilford Press, 1993).

8. Albert Ellis, John F. McInerney, Raymond DiGiuseppe, and Raymond J. Yeager, *Rational Emotive Therapy with Alcoholics and Substance Abusers* (Pergamon Press, 1988).

9. NIAAA—National Institute on Alcohol Abuse and Alcoholism, Alcoholism Report No. 33: *Neuroscience Research and Medications Development*, PH 366, July 1996.

10. Merlene Miller, Terence T. Gorski, and David K. Miller, *Learning to Live Again: A Guide to Recovery from Alcoholism* (Independence, MO: Independence Press, 1982), 123–128.

11. Terence T. Gorski, *The Developmental Model of Recovery: A Workshop Manual* (Hazel Crest, IL: The CENAPS Corporation, 1985).

12. Terence T. Gorski, *Passages through Recovery: An Action Plan for Preventing Relapse* (Center City, MN: Hazelden, 1989).

13. James O. Prochaska, John C. Norcross, and Carlo C. DiClemente, *Changing for Good* (New York: Wiliam Morrow and Company, 1994).

14. Stephanie Brown, *Treating the Alcoholic: A Development Model of Recovery* (New York: John Wiley and Sons, 1985).

15. G. A. Marlatt, and J. R. Gordon, eds., *Relapse Prevention: Maintenance Strategies in the Treatment of Addictive Behavior* (New York: Guilford Press, 1988).

16. Dennis C. Daley and G. Alan Marlatt, "Relapse Prevention"; IN EDS: Joyce H. Lowinson, Pedro Ruiz, Robert B. Millman, and John G. Langrod, *Substance Abuse: A Comprehensive Textbook* (Baltimore, MD: Williams & Wilkins, 1997).

17. J. E. Irvin, C. A. Bowers, M. E. Dunn, and M. C. Wang, "Efficacy of Relapse Prevention: A Meta-Analytic Review," *Journal of Consulting and Clinical Psychology*, Source ID: 67(3)(1999), 563–570.

18. Terence T. Gorski, "The CENAPS® Model of Relapse Prevention Planning," in Dennis W. Daly, *Relapse: Conceptual, Research, and Clinical Perspectives* (Hayworth Press, 1989), 153–161; *Journal of Chemical Dependency Treatment*, vol. 2, no. 2, 1989.
19. G. A. Marlatt and J. R. Gordon, eds., *Relapse Prevention: Maintenance Strategies in the Treatment of Addictive Behavior* (New York: Guilford Press, 1988), 351–416.
20. William H. George, "Marlatt and Gordon's Relapse Prevention Model: A Cognitive-Behavioral Approach to Understanding and Preventing Relapse," *Journal of Chemical Dependency Treatment*, vol. 2, no. 2 (1989), 153–169.
21. Caryl Trotter, *Double Bind: Recovery and Relapse Prevention for the Chemically Dependent Sexual Abuse Survivor* (Independence, MO: Herald House/Independence Press, 1992).

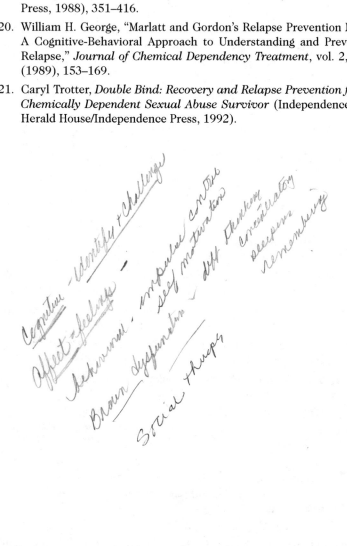

Part 2

2.1 The Conceptual Models of the GORSKI-CENAPS® System

The GORSKI-CENAPS® System is built around three primary conceptual models: a Biopsychosocial Model of Addiction, a Developmental Model of Recovery, and a Relapse Prevention Model.

2.2 Biopsychosocial Model of Addiction

The GORSKI-CENAPS® Model for Relapse Prevention Therapy is a clinical system that integrates the disease model of chemical dependency and abstinence-based counseling methods with recent advances in cognitive, affective, behavioral, and social therapies. The method is designed to be delivered across levels of care with a primary focus on outpatient delivery systems.

Addiction As a Primary Disorder: The GORSKI-CENAPS® Model is based on a biopsychosocial model that states chemical dependency is a primary disease or disorder resulting in abuse of, addiction to, and dependence on mind-altering chemicals. Long-term use of mood-altering chemicals causes brain dysfunction that disorganizes personality and causes social and occupational problems.

Brain Dysfunction: Brain dysfunction occurs during periods of intoxication, short-term withdrawal, and long-term withdrawal. Patients with a genetic history of addiction appear to be more susceptible to this brain dysfunction. As the addiction progresses, the symptoms of this brain dysfunction cause difficulty in thinking clearly, managing feelings and emotions, remembering things, sleeping restfully, recognizing and managing stress, and psychomotor coordination. The symptoms are most severe during the first six to eighteen months of sobriety, but there is a lifelong tendency for these symptoms to return during times of physical or psychosocial stress.

Personality Disorganization: Personality disorganization occurs because the brain dysfunction interferes with normal thinking, feeling, and acting. Some of the personality disorganization is temporary and will spontaneously subside with abstinence as the brain recovers from the dysfunction. Other personality traits will become deeply habituated during the addiction and will require treatment in order to subside.

Social Dysfunction: Social dysfunction—including family, work, legal, and financial problems—emerges as a consequence of brain dysfunction and resultant personality disorganization.

Goal of Treatment: The GORSKI-CENAPS® Model is based on the belief that total abstinence plus personality and lifestyle change is essential for full recovery. People raised in dysfunctional families often develop self-defeating personality styles (which AA calls character defects) that interfere with their ability to recover. Addiction is a chronic disease that has a tendency toward relapse. Relapse is the process of becoming dysfunctional in recovery that ends in physical or emotional collapse, suicide, or self-medication with alcohol or drugs. The GORSKI-CENAPS® Model incorporates the role of brain dysfunction, personality disorganization, social dysfunction, and family-of-origin problems to the problems of recovery and relapse.

Addiction and Personality: Addiction can be influenced, not caused, by self-defeating personality traits that result from being raised in a dysfunctional family. Personality is the habitual way of thinking, feeling, acting, and relating to others that develops in childhood and is unconsciously perpetuated in adult living. Personality develops as a result of an interaction between genetically inherited traits and family environment.

Being raised in a dysfunctional family can result in self-defeating personality traits or disorders. These traits and disorders do not cause the addiction to occur. They can cause a more rapid progression of the addiction, make it difficult to recognize and seek treatment during the early stages of the addiction, or make it difficult to benefit from treatment. Self-defeating personality traits and disorders also increase the risk of relapse. As a result, family-of-origin problems need to be appropriately addressed in treatment.

Drug-Based and Abstinence-Based Symptoms: The disease is a double-edged sword with two cutting edges—drug-based symptoms that manifest themselves during active episodes of chemical use and sobriety-based symptoms that emerge during periods of abstinence. The abstinence-based symptoms create a tendency toward relapse that is part of the disease itself.

Relapse Syndrome: The relapse syndrome is an integral part of the addictive disease process. Relapse is the process of becoming dysfunctional in sobriety due to sobriety-based symptoms that lead to either renewed alcohol or drug use, physical or emotional collapse, or suicide. The relapse process is marked by predictable and identifiable warning signs that begin long before alcohol and drug use or collapse occurs. Relapse Prevention Therapy teaches patients to recognize and manage these warning signs and to interrupt the relapse progression early and return to positive progress in recovery.

Biopsychosocial Model of Treatment: The GORSKI-CENAPS® Biopsychosocial Model is a tightly integrated and complete system for biopsychosocial assessment and treatment. This biopsychosocial perspective makes the GORSKI-CENAPS® Model an excellent tool for integrating the efforts of multidisciplinary treatment teams. The GORSKI-CENAPS® Model integrates biological interventions such as detoxification and medication management; psychological interventions based on cognitive, affective, and behavioral methods; social and cultural interventions such as family therapy, employment counseling, legal counseling, and financial counseling.

2.3 Developmental Model of Recovery

The GORSKI-CENAPS® Developmental Model of Recovery is based on the belief that addiction and its related mental and personality disorders are chronic lifestyle-related conditions that require a long-term developmental process of recovery. This model is very similar to the research model of Stephanie Brown and Prochasca. The CENAPS® developmental recovery process is conceptualized as moving through a series of six stages.

Stage 0—Active Addiction: During this stage substance abusers are actively using alcohol and other drugs, receiving substantial perceived benefits from their use, experiencing few perceived adverse consequences, and as a result see no reason to seek treatment.

Stage 1—Transition: During the *Transition Stage* the primary focus is on interrupting denial and treatment resistance.

Stage 2—Stabilization: During the *Stabilization Stage* the primary focus is on breaking the addiction cycle, managing withdrawal, stabilizing mental status, and managing situational life crises.

Stage 3—Early Recovery: During the *Early Recovery Stage* the primary focus is on teaching patients about addiction and its related mental and personality disorders, teaching them about the recovery process, helping them establish a structured recovery program, and teaching basic skills for identifying and changing addictive thoughts, feelings, and behaviors to sobriety-centered thoughts, feelings, and behaviors.

Stage 4—Middle Recovery: During the *Middle Recovery Stage* the primary focus is on repairing damage caused by the addiction to significant others in the areas of work, social, intimate, and friendship systems and to develop a balanced and healthy lifestyle.

Stage 5—Late Recovery: During *Late Recovery* the focus is on helping the person make changes in self-defeating personality styles and self-defeating lifestyle structures that interfere with maintaining sobriety and responsibility. During this stage the person needs to deal with family-of-origin issues, which impair the quality of recovery and act as long-term relapse triggers.

Stage 6—Maintenance: During the *Maintenance Stage* the primary focus is on the maintenance of sobriety and responsibility while actively participating in the developmental life process so as not to slip back into old addictive patterns.

2.4 Relapse Prevention Model

The GORSKI-CENAPS® Relapse Prevention Model is designed to reduce the frequency, duration, and severity of relapse episodes by teaching clients to identify and manage high-risk situations that cause relapse in early recovery and the core personality and lifestyle problems that contribute to relapse later in recovery after initial stabilization has been achieved. There is also a Relapse Early Intervention component designed to stop relapse quickly should it occur and get the person back into a treatment and recovery program.

Relapse Prevention: Clients are taught to prevent relapse by using three specific methods: *(1) Relapse Prevention Counseling (RPC),* which teaches clients to identify and manage the high-risk situations that can activate craving or cause an immediate relapse; *(2) Relapse Prevention Therapy (RPT),* which teaches clients to identify and manage the core personality and lifestyle problems that cause unnecessary stress, pain, and problems in recovery; and (3) *Relapse Early Intervention,* which teaches clients to stop relapse quickly, should it occur, by using Relapse Early Intervention methods.

2.5 Cognitive, Affective, Behavioral, Social (CABS) Therapy

The GORSKI-CENAPS® Model of Relapse Management is based on a balanced biopsychosocial model that recognizes five primary psychological domains and three primary social domains of functioning.

Primary Psychological Systems

- Consciousness System (regulates self-awareness)
- Cognitive System (regulates thinking)
- Affective System (regulates feeling and emotion)

- Imagery System (regulates imagination or sensory image formation) as it applies to the personal time line (past, present, and future)

- Behavioral System (regulates motivation and action). Imagery is viewed as a primary mediating function between thinking, feeling, and acting. The GORSKI-CENAPS® Model for Relapse Prevention Therapy makes extensive use of both guided imagery for mental rehearsal and spontaneous imagery for cognitive and emotional integration work.

Primary Social Systems: The primary social domains are: (1) work, (2) friendship, and (3) intimate relationships.

Preferred Modes of Psychosocial Functioning: People usually have a preference for one psychological and one social domain. These preferred domains become overdeveloped while the others remain underdeveloped. The goal is to reinforce the skills in the overdeveloped domains while focusing the client on building skills in the underdeveloped domains. The goal is to achieve healthy, balanced functioning.

Each of these domains is considered equally important, and the clinical goal is to help patients achieve competent functioning within each of these three domains.

Standard Treatment Modalities: The GORSKI-CENAPS® Model for Relapse Prevention Therapy incorporates the use of standard and structured group and individual therapy sessions and psychoeducation programs that focus the patients' attention primarily on these five primary goals. The treatment is holistic in nature and involves the patients in a structured program of recovery activities. Willingness to comply with the recovery structure and actively participate within the structured sessions is a major factor in accepting patients for treatment with this model.

Agent of Change: The primary agent of change is the completion of a structured clinical protocol in a process-oriented interaction between the patient, the primary therapist or counselor, and members of the therapy groups.

2.6 Treatment-Planning Components

The GORSKI-CENAPS® Model consists of six interrelated *treatment-planning components*. Each of these components addresses a common issue that is frequently the central focus of treatment. When combined together, these components provide effective guidelines that address 80 percent of the treatment issues raised by clients in recovery from noncomplicated cases of addiction. The six treatment planning components are listed below:

Component 1—Assessment and Treatment Planning (ATP): The primary focus is recognizing addiction and related personality and mental disorders. This component presents general guidelines for (1) completing a comprehensive assessment for addiction and related personality disorders, mental disorders, and situational life problems and (2) developing a brief strategic treatment plan that appropriately matches clients to one of the following treatment planning components. The selected treatment planning component is then customized to meet the individualized needs of the client.

The goals of Assessment and Treatment Planning (ATP) are to

- identify substance use disorders, mental disorders, personality disorders, and situational life problems;
- write a prioritized list;
- develop a short-term brief strategic treatment plan;
- create a long-term recovery vision; and
- refer client to the next appropriate type of treatment.

Component 2—Denial Management Counseling (DMC): The primary focus is managing denial and resistance. This component presents a master treatment plan for interrupting denial, overcoming treatment resistance, and motivating participation in treatment.

The goals of Denial Management Counseling (DMC) are to
- stop denial and resistance and
- refer for Primary Recovery Counseling (PRC).

Component 3—Primary Recovery Counseling (PRC): The primary focus is learning basic recovery skills. This component presents a master treatment plan for developing a structured recovery program and teaching foundational recovery skills needed for breaking the addiction cycle and maintaining abstinence.

The goals of Primary Recovery Counseling (PRC) are to
- teach foundational recovery skills and
- refer for Relapse Prevention Therapy (RPT).

Component 4—Relapse Prevention Counseling (RPC): The primary focus is managing high-risk situations. This component presents a master treatment plan for identifying and managing high-risk situations that can cause relapse.

The goals of Relapse Prevention Counseling (RPC) are to
- identify and manage high-risk situations that cause relapse and
- refer to the next appropriate type of treatment.

Component 5—Relapse Prevention Therapy (RPT): The primary focus is managing core personality and lifestyle problems. This component presents a master treatment plan for identifying and changing core personality and lifestyle problems that create stress, pain, and problems that can lead to relapse later in recovery after initial abstinence has been achieved.

The goals of Relapse Prevention Therapy (RPT) are to
- identify and manage core personality and lifestyle issues and
- refer for Ongoing Case Management (OCM): The primary focus of Ongoing Case Management is to provide support, monitoring, and access to early intervention.

Component 6—Dual Disorders Counseling (DDC): The primary focus is managing addiction-related mental and personality disorders. This component presents a set of guidelines for integrating the treatment of addiction and the related mental disorders and personality disorders that often lead to relapse if left untreated.

2.7 Helping Characteristics

Effective therapists have integrated eight basic helping characteristics into their personalities. Their effectiveness will improve as they consistently demonstrate a broader balance of these characteristics.

In the GORSKI-CENAPS® Model these helping characteristics are also applied in group therapy. Since an important role of group members is to help one another solve problems, it seems reasonable that the higher the level of helping characteristics demonstrated by group members during sessions, the more effective the groups will be. This establishes a primary goal of the group leader to encourage the development of helping characteristics in all group members by role modeling these characteristics.

1. Empathy: the ability to understand how another person perceives or experiences a situation or event. It is the ability to enter the context, mind-set, or frame of reference of another person and perceive the world from his or her point of view. It is also the ability to communicate your perception of how the other person perceives the experience.

2. Genuineness: the ability to be fully yourself and express your unique individual style and personality to another. It is an absence of phoniness, role playing, and defensiveness. In a genuine person the outer behavior (the public self) matches the inner thoughts and feelings (the private self).

3. Respect: the ability to communicate to another person, both verbally and nonverbally, the belief that they have the inner strength and capacity to make it in life, to make their own decisions, and to learn from the consequences of those decisions.

4. Self-Disclosure: the ability to communicate personal thoughts, feelings, attitudes, and beliefs to another person in a context-appropriate manner when it is for the benefit of the other person for you to do so.

5. **Warmth:** a nonverbal behavior that demonstrates positive regard and makes another person psychologically visible in a positive way. Examples of behavior that communicate warmth would be touching, smiling, making eye contact, talking in a soft, gentle tone of voice, etc.

6. **Immediacy:** the ability to focus on the "here and now" interaction between yourself and other people. The use of "I" statements followed by statements of personal reaction typically express immediacy. Examples would be: "Right now I am feeling _____. When you said that, I began to think _____. Right now I feel like _____. As you were speaking, I began to sense that you were experiencing _____."

7. **Concreteness:** the ability to identify and clarify particular problems or issues. It also includes the ability to design an action plan that describes the specific steps that need to be solved in order to correct or resolve the problem. Concreteness involves the ability to keep focused on a specific problem and the action plan designed to resolve it. It includes making clear expectations of others and inspecting the outcomes of those expectations.

8. **Confrontation:** the act of honestly communicating to another person your perception of reality that includes your honest perception of the person's strengths and weaknesses; what you believe the person is thinking and feeling; how you observe the person to be acting; and what you believe are the logical consequences of those actions. Effective confrontation communicates your view of reality to the other person in a way that supports the person while pointing out self-defeating thinking, emotional responses, behavior, and situational involvement.

2.8 Interviewing Skills

There are seven core therapeutic communication techniques that are used when implementing all GORSKI-CENAPS® treatment plans.

1. **Focused Questioning:** an interviewing skill that involves developing and using a sequence of open-ended questions to guide the patient in a systematic process of self-exploration. In DMC the goals of the focused questioning sequences are to interrupt denial and resistance, recognize and accept the reality of the substance use disorder, and motivate the client to voluntarily move on to the next phase of treatment.

2. **Active Listening:** an interviewing skill that involves asking a focused question, listening carefully to the answer, using same-word feedback with an accuracy check, using other word feedback (paraphrasing) with an accuracy check, and moving on to the next question. If used properly, active listening helps clients feel listened to, understood, taken seriously, and affirmed.

3. **Immediate Relaxation Response Training:** an interviewing skill that focuses on keeping stress levels low while exploring difficult issues. It involves teaching clients to use a subjective stress thermometer to self-monitor stress levels, contracting for time-outs if either the client or the therapist sense stress levels are getting too high, and using brief relaxation techniques to immediately lower the stress to functional levels.

4. **Sentence Completion:** an interviewing skill that allows clients to quickly identify and clarify core issues by completing a sentence stem multiple times and then selecting and creating new sentence stems from the hot responses on the first sentence completion list.

5. **Sentence Repetition:** an interviewing skill that allows clients to quickly identify strong feelings, memories, and future fantasies related to specific self-talk statements. This skill involves listening for the automatic self-talk associated with hot responses during an interview, making the core activating statement explicit in a sentence, and asking the client to repeat the sentence while self-

monitoring for self-talk, strong feelings, action urges, and emerging denial patterns.

6. Inner Dialogue: an interviewing skill that is used to help a client identify and clarify the components of internal dissonance. Most addicted people have an inner conflict between *the addictive irresponsible self*, the part of the person that believes that the use of alcohol, drugs, and irresponsible behaviors is good for them; and *the sober responsible self*, the part of the person that recognizes the problems with alcohol, drugs and irresponsible behaviors. The inner dialogue technique asks a person to identify the battle between these two sides of their personality and learn how to engage in conscious dialogue and train the sober responsible self to win the arguments.

7. Bookmarking: an interviewing skill that identifies and clarifies secondary problems, writes down the problem issues, and formally defers the problem until later in therapy by showing how trying to deal with the problem now would interfere with accomplishing the primary goal of the current treatment.

2.9 Treatment Delivery Systems

The GORSKI-CENAPS® Model can use one of three treatment delivery systems: Pyschoeducation Programs, Problem-Solving Group Therapy, and Individual Therapy.

Delivery System 1—Pyschoeducation Programs: These programs teach recovery skills to large groups of clients using an experiential adult learning model. A standard psychoeducation group format is used that is based on proven adult learning principles.

Pretest: Participants are given a pretest to determine their knowledge level at the beginning of the sessions.

Lecture: A brief lecture is given describing basic information for the class.

Group Exercise: A group learning exercise is completed that requires all class members to become actively involved in using the material they heard in the lecture.

Posttest: Participants are given a posttest to see if they changed any of their answers as a result of the sessions.

Discussion: The instructor facilitates a group discussion and question and answer session as he or she reviews with the class the correct answers to the test.

Delivery System 2—Problem-Solving Group Therapy: Problem-Solving Group Therapy allows each client to systematically implement the action steps in their treatment plan in a structured support group setting.

The GORSKI-CENAPS® Model for Relapse Prevention Therapy uses a standard session model of problem-solving group therapy that consists of group rules, group responsibilities, a standard group format, and a standard problem-solving procedure.

Group Rules: The following rules are used as part of the problem-solving group process:

- Say anything you want, any time you want to say it. Silence is not a virtue in this group and can be harmful to your recovery.

- Refuse to answer any question or participate in any activity except the basic group responsibilities. The group cannot force you to participate, but members do have the right to express how they feel about your silence or your choice not to get involved.

- Confidentiality: What happens in the group stays among the members, with the exception of the counselors who may consult with other counselors to provide more effective treatment.

- No violence. No swearing, putting down, physical violence, or threats of violence. The threat of violence is as good as the act.

- No dating, romantic involvement, or sexual involvement among the members of the group. Such activities can sabotage group members' treatment. If such involvement starts to develop, bring it to the attention of the group or your individual counselor at once.

- Anyone who decides to leave group treatment has a responsibility to inform the group in person, prior to termination.

- Group sessions are two hours in duration. Patients should be on time and should plan not to leave the session before it is over. Smoking, eating, and drinking beverages are not allowed in group.

Group Responsibilities: Group members agree to fulfill the following basic group responsibilities:

- Give a reaction at the beginning of each session.
- Volunteer to work on a personal issue in each group session.
- Complete all assignments and report to the group what was learned from completing them.
- Listen to other group members when they present problems.
- Ask questions to help clarify the problem or proposed solution.
- Give feedback about how you see the problem and how you feel about the group member presenting the problem.
- Share personal experiences with similar problems when appropriate.
- Complete the closure exercise by reporting to the group what you learned in the session and what you will do differently as a result of what you learned.

Problem-Solving Group Counseling Format: The group therapy sessions follow a standard eight-part group therapy protocol. The first and last steps of the protocol (preparation and debriefing sessions) are attended by the therapy team only. The other steps in the protocol occur during the group therapy session itself.

1. **Preparation Session:** The preparation session begins by reviewing patients' treatment plans, goals, and current progress in implementing treatment interventions. Each patient's progress is reviewed, and an attempt is made to predict the assignments and problems that the patient will present.

2. **Opening Procedure:** (5 minutes) During the opening procedure, the counselor sets the climate for the group, establishes leadership, and helps patients warm up to the group process.

3. **Reactions to Last Session:** (15 minutes) A reaction is a brief description of (1) what each group member thought during the last group session, (2) how the group member felt during the last group session, and (3) the identification of the three persons who stood out from the last session and why they were remembered.

4. **Report on Assignments:** (10 minutes) Assignments are exercises where patients are working to identify and manage relapse warning signs or deal with other problems related to relapse prevention. Some of these assignments will be completed in group. Others will need to be completed between group sessions.

Immediately following reactions, the counselor will ask all group members who have received assignments to briefly answer six questions: (1) What was the assignment and why was it assigned? (2) Was the assignment completed and, if not, what happened when you tried to do it? (3) What was learned from the completion of the assignment? (4) What feelings and emotions were experienced while completing the assignment? (5) Did any issues surface that will require additional work in group? (6)

Is there anything else that you want to work on in group today?

5. **Setting the Agenda:** (3 minutes) When all assignments have been reported on, the group counselor will identify all persons who want to work and announce who and in what order people will work. Group members who do not have time to present their work in this group session will be first on the agenda in the following group session. It is best to plan on having no more than three patients working in any group session.

6. **Problem-Solving Group Process:** (70 minutes) The problem-solving group process is designed to allow patients to present issues to the group, clarify these issues through group questioning, receive feedback from the group, receive feedback from the counselor (if appropriate), and develop assignments for continued progress.

7. **Closure Exercise:** (15 minutes) When there is approximately fifteen minutes left in the group session, the group therapist will ask each member to report what is the most important thing they learned in group and what they are going to do differently as a result of what they learned.

8. **Debriefing Session:** The debriefing session is designed to review the patient's problems and progress, prevent counselor burnout, and improve the group skills of the counselor. If this can be done with other counselors running similar groups, it is especially helpful. A brief review of each patient is completed, outstanding group members and events are identified, progress and problems discussed, and the personal feelings and reactions of the counselor are reviewed.

Standard Problem-Solving Process: Group therapy participants learn a standard Problem-Solving Group Process that guides problem resolution. The seven-step process follows:

1. **Problem Identification:** First, have the members ask questions to identify what is causing difficulty. *What is the problem?*

2. **Problem Clarification:** Encourage patients to be specific and complete. *Is this the real problem or is there a more fundamental one?*

3. **Identification of Alternatives:** *What are some options for dealing with the problem?* Ask patients to list them on paper so they can readily see them. Try to have the group come up with a list of at least five possible solutions. This will give them more of a chance of choosing the best solution and give them some alternatives if their first choice doesn't work.

4. **Projected Consequences of Each Alternative:** *What are the best, worst, and most likely outcomes that could be achieved by using each alternative solution?*

5. **Decision:** Have the group ask the person which option offers the best outcome and seems to have the best chance for success. Ask them to make a decision based on the alternatives they have.

6. **Action:** Once they have decided on a solution to the problem, they need to plan how they will carry it out. The plan should answer the question: *What are you going to do about it?* A plan is a road map to achieve a goal. There are short-range goals and long-range goals. Long-range goals are achieved along with short-range goals—one step at a time.

7. **Follow-Up:** Ask patients to carry out their plans and report how they are working.

Delivery System 3—Individual Therapy: Individual therapy allows clients to systematically implement the action steps in their treatment plan in individual sessions. These individual therapy sessions can be used as an exclusive mode of treatment or used in conjunction with psychoeducation and problem-solving group therapy.

The goal of individual therapy is to assist patients in identifying and clarifying problems and preparing to present them in group. A standard agenda is used:

- **Reactions to Last Session:** The therapist discusses patients' reactions to the last individual and group therapy session.

- **Sobriety Check:** The therapist asks patients if they have been clean and sober, if they have experienced any cravings or urges to use alcohol or drugs, if they have attended all scheduled recovery activities, and how they feel about attending those activities.

- **Clinical Work:** The issues patients are currently working on are reviewed in depth. During this part of the session the therapist will present problem identification and clarification work and motivate patients to present issues in group. If intense cathartic work is required, this is usually done in individual sessions rather than in group therapy sessions.

- **Preparation for Group:** Patients rehearse how they will present issues to the group. The primary goal of individual therapy is to prepare and support patients in efficiently working on issues in group. Group is viewed as the primary or central treatment modality with individual therapy playing a supportive role.

Delivery System 4—Family Treatment: The GORSKI-CENAPS® Model has a family treatment component that involves communication and intervention training around the developing warning signs and relapse early intervention training. It allows the patient and family member to have a concrete behavioral response should alcohol and drug use recur.

Family therapy is normally delivered in a *parallel model*. The patient is involved in individual and group therapy for recovery from chemical dependency, and the family members (especially the spouse or intimate partner) are encouraged to enter individual and group therapy for the treatment of codependency and other personal issues. Sessions are established to work with specific couples and family communication training and problem solving. Special emphasis is placed on developing open communication around recovery goals, relapse warning signs for both chemical dependency and codependency, family warning sign identification and management skills, and family intervention planning should alcohol and drug use or acting out codependent behavior occur.

The goal of family therapy is to remove the chemically dependent partner from the identified patient role and create a family recovery focus where each family member needs to initiate a personal recovery program for chemical dependency or codependency. The family needs to establish a family recovery plan for improving the overall functioning of the family system.

Family therapy is viewed as important but adjunctive to relapse prevention therapy. Many relapse-prone patients do not have a committed family system, and many family members refuse to become involved in therapy because of the long history of past failure. Many relapse-prone patients can and do achieve long-term recovery with the GORSKI-CENAPS® Model for Relapse Prevention Therapy, even though the family is not involved in treatment.

Delivery System 5—Self-Help Groups: Related self-help groups provide ongoing support and peer assistance while implementing the action steps in their treatment plans. The GORSKI-CENAPS® Model is compatible with many support groups including Twelve-Step programs based on Alcoholics Anonymous (AA) and MISA (Mentally Ill Substance Abusers).

Because it is based on a disease model and abstinence-based treatment, the GORSKI-CENAPS® Model is designed to be compatible with Twelve-Step programs. A special interpretation of the Twelve Steps was developed to help patients relate Twelve-Step program involvement to relapse prevention principles.

Special self-help support groups, called Relapse Prevention Support Groups, were developed to encourage patients to continue in ongoing warning-sign identification and management. These Relapse Prevention Support Groups can be set up to allow clients to gain low-cost peer support while completing specific types of treatment plans.

Delivery System 6—Multimodality Programs: Most treatment programs are multimodality in nature. They use a variety of related clinical models and delivery systems. The GORSKI-CENAPS® Model has been used successfully in the context of a wide variety of multimodality programs directed at a wide variety of special populations.

2.10 Strategies for Dealing with Common Clinical Problems

The GORSKI-CENAPS® Model relies heavily upon structured program procedures. The process is initiated with patient contracting, and a commitment is secured for attendance, punctuality, willingness to comply with patient responsibilities, and active participation within the session structures. Patients who refuse to make such a commitment are viewed as poor candidates for the program and are not admitted for therapy.

Despite this initial participation contract, routine problems do develop in treatment. All such problems are viewed as relapse warning indicators, because they place the patient's ongoing therapy at risk and, hence, increase the risk of relapse. The following issues are promptly dealt with as critical issues:

Lateness: Patients are expected to be on time for sessions. In group, the standard procedure for dealing with lateness is as follows: (1) Before entering group, patients contract to be on time for all sessions. (2) If patients arrive late within the first fifteen minutes of group (prior to the end of reactions), they are allowed to stay for that group session only if they agree to work on the issues that prompted their lateness. (3) If patients are more than fifteen minutes late for the first session or less than fifteen minutes late for the second session, they are not allowed in group. They must have an individual session with their therapist before being allowed back in group and produce evidence that they have identified and resolved the issues related to their lateness. (4) If patients are late on three or more occasions during any twelve-week period of time, they are discharged from group.

Similar no-nonsense procedures are applied to group therapy and individual therapy. Only extremely credible excuses are honored for absence or tardiness, and this is only if they have not developed a pattern of absence or tardiness.

Missed Sessions: Patients are expected to attend all therapy sessions. The only excuse for absence is documented extreme illness (with a physician's note) and documented serious life crisis, such as death in the family. All excused absences must be telephoned in and must be approved by the therapist in advance. Any pattern of three or more absences within any twelve-week period is grounds for dismissal regardless of the reasons.

Chemical Relapse and Intoxicated Patients: Intoxicated patients are not allowed to remain in group. If the therapist or group members suspect intoxication, the patient is asked to verify it in group. If the patient denies intoxication, but their behavior gives reasonable cause to believe he or she has been using alcohol or drugs, they are immediately given a breath test for alcohol and a urine drug screen.

Appearing intoxicated for session is viewed as a chemical relapse. The patient is immediately removed from group because he or she will be disruptive and cannot benefit from therapy when under the influence of mood-altering drugs. An immediate screening appointment is established, and the patient is admitted to a stabilization program at the appropriate level of care to deal with withdrawal.

The therapist deals with relapse to alcohol and drug use as a medical issue requiring stabilization and treats the patient professionally. Anger at the patient is viewed as a maladaptive counter-transference response, and the therapist needs to resolve that issue in clinical supervision.

Patient refusal to follow recommendations for stabilization, results in termination from treatment. If patients follow stabilization recommendations, they are evaluated at the end of stabilization and are referred to appropriate ongoing treatment. This usually involves being returned to the same therapist and outpatient group to process the relapse and use material learned to update and revise relapse prevention strategies.

In short, relapse is viewed as part of the disease and is dealt with nonjudgmentally and nonpunitively. The relapse is processed so it can become a learning experience for the patient.

Denial, Resistance, and Poor Motivation: The GORSKI-CENAPS® Model views resistance on a continuum from simple denial of chemical dependency to delusion states based on cognitive impairments or severe personality pathology. The underlying cause of the denial is assessed and special treatment interventions are set up to deal with it.

Since patients in severe and rigid denial are inappropriate candidates for relapse prevention therapy, they are referred to transitional counseling programs that are designed to deal with patients with high levels of denial and treatment resistance. Once patients become treatment ready, they can reapply for admission to the Relapse Prevention Therapy Program.

Crisis during Treatment: Crisis situations are viewed as critical relapse warning signs. The implementation of the standard treatment plan is discontinued and special crisis management procedures are implemented to stabilize the crisis. Once the crisis is stabilized, the patient is reassessed, the treatment plan is updated, and the patient returns to working on standard relapse prevention tasks as outlined in the treatment plan.

If possible, the crisis is stabilized in the context of the GORSKI-CENAPS® Model for Relapse Prevention Therapy. If the crisis is so severe that it interferes with the patient's ability to be involved, he or she is transferred to another type or level of care to focus on the crisis stabilization.

The GORSKI-CENAPS® Corporation

The GORSKI-CENAPS® Corporation is a training, consultation, and international networking organization committed to the development and dissemination of a unified model for the treatment of substance use disorders and related personality disorders, mental disorders, and lifestyle problems.

Mission: By the year 2010 all people will have access to affordable resources for developing effective recovery and relapse prevention plans.

Vision: Better treatment will be available to more people at a lower cost. All people, no matter how sick, will have the opportunity to recover. No person or group of persons will be thrown away in the name of cost containment. A unified no-nonsense model of treatment that integrates the most advanced biological, cognitive, affective, behavioral, and social therapies will be fully operational. This model will be the recognized standard in the treatment of substance use disorders, mental disorders, personality disorders, and situational life problems.

References

The following references influenced the development of the GORSKI-CENAPS® Model for Relapse Prevention Therapy:

Annis, H. M. 1990. Effective treatment for drug and alcohol problems: What do we know? *Substance Abuse and Corrections*, Vol. 2, No. 4.

Beck, Aaron T., Fred D. Wright, Cory F. Newman, and Bruce S. Liese. 1993. *Cognitive Therapy of Substance Abuse*. New York: Guilford Press.

Berke, J. D., and S. E. Hyman. 2000. Addiction, dopamine, and the molecular mechanisms of memory. *Neuron* 25: 515–532. http://www.neuron.org/cgi/content/full/25/3/515/.

Brown, Stephanie. 1985. *Treating the Alcoholic: A Development Model of Recovery*. New York: John Wiley & Sons.

Daley, Dennis C., and G. Alan Marlatt. 1997. Relapse Prevention; IN: EDS: Joyce H. Lowinson, Pedro Ruiz, Robert B. Millman, and John G. Langrod. *Substance Abuse: A Comprehensive Textbook*. Baltimore, MD: Williams & Wilkins.

Ellis, Albert, John F. McInerney, Raymond DiGiuseppe, and Raymond J. Yeager. 1988. *Rational Emotive Therapy with Alcoholics and Substance Abusers*. Pergamon Press.

Garavan, H., J. Pankiewicz, A. Bloom, J. K. Cho, L. Sperry, T.J. Ross, B.J. Salmeron, R. Risinger, D. Kelley, and E. A. Stein. 2000. Cue-Induced cocaine craving: Neuroanatomical specificity for drug users and drug stimuli. *American Journal of Psychiatry* 157: 1789–1798. http://ajp.psychiatryonline.org/cgi/content/full/157/11/1789.

Gorski, T. September 1976. *The Dynamics of Relapse in the Alcoholic Patient*. Harvey, Illinois: Ingalls Memorial Hospital.

Gorski, T. 1980. Dynamics of relapse. *EAP Digest*. 16–21, 45–49.

Gorski, T., and M. Miller. 1982. *Counseling for Relapse Prevention*. Independence, MO: Herald House/ Independence Press.

Gorski, T., and M. Miller. 1986. *Staying Sober: A Guide for Relapse Prevention*. Independence, MO: Herald House/ Independence Press.

Gorski, T. Fall 1986. Relapse prevention planning: A new recovery tool. *Alcohol Health and Research World*. 6–11, 63.

Gorski, T. 1988. *The Staying Sober Workbook: A Serious Solution for the Problem of Relapse*. Independence, MO: Herald House/Independence Press.

Gorski, T. 1989. *How to Start Relapse Prevention Support Groups*. Independence, MO: Herald House/Independence Press.

Gorski, T. 1989. *The Relapse Recovery Grid*. Center City, MN: Hazeldon.

Miller, M., and T. Gorski. 1989. *Staying Sober Recovery Education Modules*. Independence, MO: Herald House/Independence Press.

Gorski, T. 1989. *The GORSKI-CENAPS® Model of relapse prevention planning. Journal of Chemical Dependency Treatment*, vol. 2, no. 2: 153–169.

Gorski, T. April–June 1990. The GORSKI-CENAPS® Model of relapse prevention: Basic principles and procedures. *Journal of Psychoactive Drugs*. 125.

Gorski, T. September/October 1990. Supervisory guidelines for counselors in relapse. *The Counselor*. 12–15.

Gorski, T., and T. Bell. March 1992. Recovery and relapse: Preventing relapse in chemically dependent adolescents. *Employee Assistance*. 29, 41–42.

Gorski, T. March/April 1992. Relapse: Not a reason to give up. *Addiction & Recovery*. 13–14.

Gorski, T. March/April 1992. Preventing relapse. *Addiction Counseling World*. 23.

Gorski, T. March/April 1992. Relapse therapy: Dual diagnosis and relapse. *The Counselor*. 48.

Gorski, T. July/August 1992. Creating a relapse prevention program in your treatment center. *Addiction & Recovery*. 16–17.

Gorski, T. July/August 1992. Relapse prevention in managed care. *Journal of Health Care Benefits*. 50–52.

Gorski, T. July/August 1992. Relapse therapy: Megatrends and relapse. *The Counselor*. 44.

Gorski, T. January/February 1993. AIDS and relapse: Why stay sober if I'm dying? *Addiction & Recovery*. 41–44.

Gorski, T. January/February 1993. Relapse early intervention training. *The Counselor* (January/February 1993): 36.

Gorski, T. 1985. *The Developmental Model of Recovery: A Workshop Manual*. Hazel Crest, IL: The CENAPS® Corporation.

Gorski, T. 1989. *Passages through Recovery: An Action Plan for Preventing Relapse*, Hazelden.

George, William H. 1989. Marlatt and Gordon's relapse prevention model: A cognitive-behavioral approach to understanding and preventing relapse, *Journal of Chemical Dependency Treatment*, vol. 2, no. 2: 153–169.

Irvin, J. E., C. A. Bowers, M. E. Dunn, and M. C. Wang. 1999. Efficacy of relapse prevention: A meta-analytic review, *Journal of Consulting and Clinical Psychology*. Source ID: 67(3): 563–570.

Leshner, A. I. Spring 2001. Addiction is a brain disease. *Issues of Science & Technology Online*. http://www.nap.edu/issues/17.3/leshner.htm.

Leshner, A. I. 1999. Science-Based views of drug addiction and its treatment. *Journal of the American Medical As-*

sociation. 282: 1314–1316. *http://jama.ama-assn.org/issues/v282n14/rfull/jct90020html.*

Marlatt, G. A., and J. R. Gordon, eds. 1988. *Relapse Prevention: Maintenance Strategies in the Treatment of Addictive Behavior.* New York: Guilford Press, 351–416.

Miller, M., T. Gorski, and D. Miller. 1980. *Learning to Live Again: A Guide for Recovery from Alcoholism.* Independence, MO: Herald House/Independence Press.

Miller, W. R., and R. J. Harris. September 2000. Simple scale of Gorski's warning signs for relapse. *Journal of Studies on Alcohol* 61(5):759–765.

McLellan, A. T., D. C. Lewis, C. P. O'Brien, and H.D. Kleber. 2000. Drug dependence: A chronic medical illness. *Journal of the American Medical Association* 284: 1689–1695. *http://jama.ama.ama-assn.org/issues/v284n13/rfull/jsc00024.html.*

NIAAA—National Institute on Alcohol Abuse and Alcoholism. July 1996. *Alcoholism Report No. 33: Neuroscience Research and Medications Development*, PH 366.

NIDA—National Institute on Drug Abuse. July 2000. *Principles of Drug Addiction Treatment: A Research-Based Guide.* Bethesda, MD: National Institutes of Health. *http://165.112.78.61/PODAT/PODATindex.html.*

NIDA—National Institute on Drug Abuse. March 1997. *Preventing Drug Use among Children and Adolescents: A Research-Based Guide.* Bethesda, MD: National Institutes of Health. *http://165.112.78.61/Prevention/Prevopen.html.*

Nestler, E. J. 2000. Genes and addiction. *Nature Genetics* 26: 277–281. *http://www.nature.com/cgi-taf/DynaPage.taf?file=/ng/journal/v26/n3/full/ng1100_277.html.*

Physician Leadership on National Drug Policy, position paper on drug policy. January 2000. PLNDP Program Office, Brown University, Providence, RI: Center for Alcohol and

Addiction Studies. *http://center.butler.brown.edu/plndp/Resources/resources.html*.

Prochaska, James O., John C. Norcross, and Carlo C. DiClemente. 1994. *Changing for Good*. New York: William Morrow and Company Inc.

Tabakoff, Boris, and Paula L. Hoffman. 1988. A neurobiological theory of alcoholism. IN: EDS: C.D. Chaudron and D.A. Wilkinson. *Theories on Alcoholism*, Toronto, Canada: Addiction Research Foundation.

Tarter, Ralph E., Arthur I. Alterman, and Kathleen L. Edwards. 1988. Neurobehavioral theory of alcoholism etiology, IN: EDS: C.D. Chaudron and D.A. Wilkinson. *Theories on Alcoholism*. Toronto, Canada: Addiction Research Foundation.

Taxman, F. S., and J. A. Bouffard. 2000. The importance of systems in improving offender outcomes: New frontiers in treatment Integrity. *Justice Research and Policy* 2: 37–58.

Trotter, Caryl. 1992. *Double Bind: Recovery and Relapse Prevention for the Chemically Dependent Sexual Abuse Survivor*. Independence, MO: Herald House/Independence Press.

Wilson, G. Terence. 1988. Alcohol use and abuse: Social learning analysis; IN: IN: EDS: C.D. Chaudron and D.A. Wilkinson. *Theories on Alcoholism*, Toronto, Canada: Addiction Research Foundation.

Notes

Cognitive = thinking
affect = feeling
behavioral = action - urges -
social -- environment - social network

Consciousness - regulates self awareness

ATP -